The Burning of the Reichstag: The History of the Controversial Fire That Led to the Rise of Nazi Germany

By Charles River Editors

The Reichstag burning on the night of February 27, 1933

About Charles River Editors

Charles River Editors provides superior editing and original writing services across the digital publishing industry, with the expertise to create digital content for publishers across a vast range of subject matter. In addition to providing original digital content for third party publishers, we also republish civilization's greatest literary works, bringing them to new generations of readers via ebooks.

[Sign up here to receive updates about free books as we publish them](), and visit [Our Kindle Author Page]() to browse today's free promotions and our most recently published Kindle titles.

Introduction

The Burning of the Reichstag (February 27, 1933)

"These sub-humans do not understand how the people stand at our side. In their mouse-holes, out of which they now want to come, of course they hear nothing of the cheering of the masses." – Hitler speaking about Communists as the Reichstag burned

"I don't care what happens in Russia! I know that the Russians pay with bills, and I should prefer to know that their bills are paid! I care about the Communist Party here in Germany and about Communist crooks who come here to set the Reichstag on fire!" – Hermann Goering

The early 1930s were a tumultuous period for German politics, even in comparison to the ongoing transition to the modern era that caused various forms of chaos throughout the rest of the world. In the United States, reliance on the outdated gold standard and an absurdly parsimonious monetary policy helped bring about the Great Depression. Meanwhile, the Empire of Japan began its ultimately fatal adventurism with the invasion of Manchuria, alienating the rest of the world with the atrocities it committed. Around the same time, Gandhi began his drive for the peaceful independence of India through nonviolent protests against the British.

It was in Germany, however, that the strongest seeds of future tragedy were sown. The struggling Weimar Republic had become a breeding ground for extremist politics, including two opposed and powerful authoritarian entities: the right-wing National Socialists and the left-wing KPD Communist Party. As the 1930s dawned, these two totalitarian groups held one another in a temporary stalemate, enabling the fragile ghost of democracy to continue a largely illusory survival for a few more years.

That stalemate was broken in dramatic fashion on a bitterly cold night in late February 1933, and it was the Nazis who emerged decisively as the victors. A single act of arson against the famous Reichstag building proved to be the catalyst that propelled Adolf Hitler to victory in the elections of March 1933, which set the German nation irrevocably on the path towards World War II. That war would plunge much of the planet into an existential battle that ultimately cost an estimated 60 million lives.

Given its importance, the burning of the Reichstag has been viewed as a turning point in history, but the mystery over who was actually responsible still lingers. Officially, a German court convicted and executed a Dutch Communist, Marinus van der Lubbe, and the Nazis would rail against the fire as a Communist plot in the ensuing weeks. Van der Lubbe claimed at trial that he acted alone, and many Communists accused the Nazis of conducting the fire as a false flag operation, but in any case, in the wake of the fire, Communists across Germany were purged, allowing Hitler and the Nazis to strengthen their hold on political power.

The Burning of the Reichstag: The History of the Controversial Fire That Led to the Rise of Nazi Germany analyzes the notorious fire that helped usher in the Nazis' rise to power in Germany. Along with pictures of important people, places, and events, you will learn about the Reichstag fire like never before, in no time at all.

The Burning of the Reichstag: The History of the Controversial Fire That Led to the Rise of Nazi Germany

About Charles River Editors

Introduction

  Chapter 1: The Reichstag Building

  Chapter 2: The Political Background Before the Arson

  Chapter 3: February 27, 1933

  Chapter 4: The Nazi Response to the Reichstag Fire

  Chapter 5: The Trial of Marinus van der Lubbe and the Other Conspirators

  Chapter 6: The Lingering Debate Over the Reichstag Fire

  Chapter 7: The Soviets and the Reichstag

  Bibliography

Chapter 1: The Reichstag Building

An illustration depicting the Reichstag circa 1900

Jürgen Matern's picture of the Reichstag in 2007

The center of the drama about to unfold in the early days of 1933 was the Reichstag building, an imposing government edifice erected in the late 19th century. The structure was built to serve as the venue for deliberations by the Parliament of the German Empire, or Reichstag, whose name was soon attached to the building itself. A palatial creation which still stands, the place has a checkered history both political and symbolic.

   A contest was held in the early 1880s for architects to submit their designs to the government in an effort to win the actual contract for planning and building the Reichstag, and Paul Wallot was the man whose blueprint was eventually chosen in 1882. Construction of the massive structure took a dozen years, with the finishing touches applied in 1894. At the same time, however, Germany's imperial family despised the structure for the whiff of democratic institutions associated with it and "sought to contain the challenge its prominence posed to the imperial palace [...] [at] its dedication, Kaiser Wilhelm II refused to allude to its purpose." (James-Chakraborty, 2000, 123). The building was originally intended to be constructed out of marble, but the imperial government balked at the cost, so a cheaper variety of stone was selected.

Wallot

An 1880 picture of the site of the Reichstag before its construction

Ultimately, the construction featured a rectangular plan that covered slightly more than 143,000 square feet. Architectural elements included Renaissance, Neo-Baroque, and Classical designs, leading some aesthetic cognoscenti of the late 19th century to feel that it was designed in poor taste. Regardless, the original exterior was heavily decorated with symbolic elements meant to represent Germany, its people, and its culture, but few of these survived World War II and the succeeding era of neglect.

The Reichstag included five entrances, known as "Portals," of which only one is made in a grand and stately style (Portal I). This entrance is fronted by a lofty portico supported by six Corinthian columns, and opens on the Platz der Republik. Though to modern eyes the Reichstag appears to be positioned quite acceptably, even its location drew criticism in earlier times because "the building's site was considered slightly unfortunate at the time because its entrance was facing the wrong side – West - with its back to the imperial Schloss and the 19th century city centre." (Berlin Online, 2014). The other four entrances are very modest, but they were used much more frequently than the main entrance in the decade leading up to World War II.

The exterior plan of the Reichstag includes four square towers, one at each corner, rising to a height of 132 feet. Two internal courtyards were also included in the design, ensuring that the structure was not simply a solid block with no interruptions. One of the most interesting external features from a historical point of view are the massive cast bronze letters mounted on the portico above Portal I, which spell out DEM DEUTSCHEN VOLKE ("The German People"). This lettering was added in 1916 at the reluctant command of Kaiser Wilhelm II, who was seeking to drum up support for his war efforts among ordinary Germans. The bronze lettering also has a more tragic tale attached to it due to the religious background of those who manufactured it, as the motto was "crafted by the highly respected firm of S.A. Loevy, founded in 1855. The Loevys were Jewish. Later, in 1938, they would secure a commission for work on Hitler's new Reich Chancellery, but in 1939 their firm would be 'aryanized,' expropriated and sold at a fire-sale price to a non-Jewish businessman. Some members of the family went into exile. Some survived the Nazis by living underground. Some were deported to the death camps and, in the name of the German people, murdered." (Hett, 2014, 10).

The Reichstag's interior consists of a ground floor and a second story. The ground floor is a labyrinth of smaller rooms with relatively pedestrian functions, such as kitchens, offices for clerks and other support personnel, and various services such as exercise rooms for the more active parliamentarians. It even included a hairdressing salon so that the politicians could easily spruce up their appearance prior to an important speech. The second story housed the grand and important chambers where the statecraft of the German Empire and the Weimar Republic was conducted.

Two major spaces dominated the second floor of the Reichstag. One of these was the 320 foot long Wandelhalle, which ran along the whole western edge of the building, on the same side as Portal I. The heart of the structure, however, in both the architectural and the functional sense, was the Plenary Chamber. This massive, cylindrical space housed the semicircular rows of seats where the Reichstag members sat during debates. The seats rose like arena seating from a focal point consisting of the president's desk, the speaker's podium, and several other desks for stenographers and other necessary personnel.

Picture of the interior

The Plenary Chamber was designed to provide excellent acoustics as well as light and air for the deputies, but ventilation was always a problem. The interior was paneled in wood to ensure the proper auditory results, and 246 feet above the floor, a huge cupola made out of glass and iron pierced the roof, providing daylight and serving to ventilate the chamber. Due to some design quirks, however, "the circulating air could only reach down to a height of about fifteen feet, the ventilation never did much for the deputies' health and alertness." (Hett, 2014, 11).

In essence, the same properties that enabled a parliamentarian's voice to be heard clearly throughout the room also made the Plenary Chamber peculiarly suited for being the victim of a fierce and uncontrollable fire. The wooden cladding on the walls provided ample fuel in a building which was otherwise mostly stone, while the chamber itself, rising vertically to an air-admitting cupola, was a giant chimney where huge updrafts would feed large amounts of oxygen to any fire. Once a blaze was started in the Plenary Chamber, extinguishing it would be problematic, particularly since it was embedded in the center of the building. The chamber's location made it that much more difficult for firefighters to reach.

In fact, the designers of the Reichstag dreaded the possibility of a fire, and for this reason, they made a fateful decision when building the edifice. Rather than placing the boilers supplying heat to the building in the parliamentary palace itself, they had constructed a "tunnel that connected the cellar of the Reichstag to the president's residence and the boiler house […] [T]his tunnel [...]

existed, ironically enough, because Reichstag architect Paul Wallot had wanted to keep the boilers away from the building to protect it against fire." (Hett, 2014, 132). At the time of the fire, the president's residence was in the possession of Hermann Goering, the newly minted president of the Reichstag and Adolf Hitler's right hand man.

Goering

The size of the Reichstag grew over the years as Germany's population increased, thanks to improved health brought on by industrialization, modern medicine, and scientific hygiene. At the time of the fire, the Reichstag often consisted of as many as 600 deputies and sometimes more, which packed even the ample Plenary Chamber to overflowing. All the while, the two Reichstags – the parliament and the eponymous building – were loathed by authoritarians of every stripe, whether they were Nazis representing the far right, the communists of the KDP, aristocratic Junkers of the old school who distrusted and despised the intelligent commoners promoted to positions of influence by democratic institutions, deeply conservative monarchists who wished to see the rule of emperors restored, or churchmen witnessing their power base and income eroded by the forces of rationalism, humanism, and free thought. Nonetheless, the Reichstag was also a convenient emblem of Germany and its people, so it could be invoked to stir up an immediate patriotic response in ordinary German citizens.

Chapter 2: The Political Background Before the Arson

After World War I, the victorious inadvertently fashioned a rod for their own backs by levying massive reparations against Germany. These extortionate claims, like most penalties that are set up to cut off every possible avenue of escape to the victim, constituted a disaster in the making. Germany was cornered by an ongoing depression from which there was no prospect of escape, keeping the people in a state of constant misery and impoverishment as the years turned into decades. Like an individual trapped by debt, poverty, and desperation who turns to a life of crime, Germany eventually turned to violence to escape the economic problems caused by the negotiations that followed the war's armistice.

In times of crisis, elections were held much more frequently than in more stable periods, but this feature of the Weimar Republic also helped ensure that any economic or political instability would be exacerbated by shifts in the governing bodies, which came at times when continuity would've been generally beneficial for keeping problems from spiraling out of control. Multiple elections occurred in close proximity to the date of the Reichstag fire, and both at the time and since, many ordinary people and historians have noted the convenient timing of the conflagration.

Unlike the U.S. Congress but similar to various European governmental councils, seats in the Reichstag were awarded on a proportional basis. For example, if a party won 20% of the vote, then it would also control 20% of the seats. This meant that at the time of the Reichstag fire, no political party held a majority. The strongest party, in numerical terms, consisted of the Social Democrats, a liberalizing force that mainly sought to increase the strength of democracy in the former German Empire. The Nazis represented a powerful bloc as well, but the number of seats they held increased when the economy faltered and decreased when a whiff of prosperity was in the air. The KDP Communists held a smaller but still significant portion of the Reichstag seats.

As might be expected, the Nazi Party and the KDP frequently worked at cross purposes, and relatively civilized feuds within the Reichstag's walls, where the leaders of the respective groups often addressed one another in highly formal and civil terms, were frequently mirrored by brutal outbreaks of violence in the streets. Once Goering became president of the Reichstag and overall leader of German police, the current of hooliganism grew stronger, sweeping Germany towards the precipice of dictatorship: "Simultaneously, the number of violent incidents and acts of anti-Semitism began to multiply significantly. The [SA and SS] began to attack the trade union and Communist offices along with the homes of their leaders but with the agreements in place with the police the common situation was that the Communists/Jews/Trade Unionists would get a kicking from the Nazis and then be arrested and thrown in prison for breaches of the peace." (Addington, 2014, Chapter 13).

The Nazis and KPD each represented, to the eyes of the people, a glimmer of hope and a way of extracting themselves from the labyrinth of poverty and humiliation the Allies had thrust them into. Though the 85 year old President Paul von Hindenburg, head of the Weimar Republic, was becoming vague at times, his Chancellor, Heinrich Brüning, clearly understood the source of Germany's woes and how these might deliver the nation into the hands of the Communists or Nazis. "During the summer the scholarly Chancellor had pondered long hours over the desperate plight of Germany. [...] To cope with the depression he had decreed lower wages and salaries as well as lower prices [...] The 'Hunger Chancellor' he had been called by both the Nazis and the Communists. Yet he thought he saw a way out that in the end would re-establish a stable, free, prosperous Germany. He would try to negotiate with the Allies a cancellation of reparations." (Shirer, 2011, 157).

Hindenburg

Brüning

 Since the Allies had failed to disarm themselves as they had bound themselves by treaty to do, Brüning also wished to rearm the German nation. Indeed, he began a secret program for a modest military expansion, which he hoped would restore Germany to equality with the other nations rather than continue to be Europe's whipping boy. This program, of course, had a very different fate; rather than being the security force that reestablished the dignity of a free people as Brüning envisioned, it would ultimately form the nucleus of Hitler's genocidal Reichswehr.

 Brüning's plan actually went even farther, as he contemplated means by which the rising power of the Nazis could be decisively and legally quashed. His solution was to create a new constitutional monarchy with strictly limited powers in Germany, but when he proposed this to Hindenburg, it was shot down forcefully by the Weimar Republic's president, not because it was too conservative but because the idea of a legally limited monarchy was too liberal for the former Imperial soldier: "When Brüning explained to [Hindenburg] that the Social Democrats and the trade unions, which [...] had given some encouragement to his plan if only because it might afford the last desperate chance of stopping Hitler, would not stand for the return of [...] Wilhelm II [...] and that moreover if the monarchy were restored it must be a constitutional and democratic one on the lines of the British model, the grizzly old Field Marshal was so outraged he summarily dismissed his Chancellor from his presence. A week later he recalled him to inform him that he would not stand for re-election." (Shirer, 2011, 158).

The next Chancellor to be appointed by Hindenburg was Franz von Papen, who practically handed Hitler the means to establish a dictatorship due to his own mistaken belief that he could easily control the man Hindenburg had dismissed contemptuously as "the Bohemian corporal." Von Papen did not last long in office, but he made the cardinal error of legalizing the SA, or Sturmabteilung, the infamous Brownshirts who served as the muscle enforcing Hitler's will on the streets. He did this in the erroneous belief that it would appease the Nazis.

Von Papen

Von Papen was almost immediately forced to resign, largely through the machinations of Hitler and allies like Goering. Economic troubles compelled the people to favor right-wing solutions, and in the disastrous days of the early 1930s, Hitler's anti-Semitism was an attractive feature to many German voters. The Jews formed an identifiable and useful scapegoat against whom to direct the rage, frustration, fear, and misery that ordinary Germans had experienced for nearly half a generation: "Germans felt the effects almost immediately. By December 1929, 1.5 million workers were unemployed. A month later, that number jumped to 2.5 million, and it kept climbing. Once again, the Nazis took advantage of a crisis by blaming everything on the Communists and the Jews. In the September 1930 election, the Nazis were expected to win 50 seats in Germany's parliament. To the surprise of many, they went from 12 seats to 107 seats." (Goldstein, 2012, 243).

Hitler's rise to power was boosted by the desperation of the Germans to extract themselves from a situation which seemingly showed no sign of a positive resolution, and his ability to appear as the champion against the forces causing Germany's troubles made him all the more popular. Since the Allies were out of reach, the helpless, vastly outnumbered Jews made an ideal substitute for the Nazis' purposes. "Hitler and other Nazis were now poised to destroy the Weimar Republic and 'restore' Germany and the 'Aryan race' to greatness by ending so-called Jewish racial domination and eliminating the Communist threat." (Goldstein, 2012, 243).

Although the Social Democrats were the overall majority party in Germany at the time, they suffered a massive disadvantage against Hitler's Nazis because they were dedicated to democratic government and were less apt to use systematic violence and intimidation to achieve their aims. The Nazis had no such scruples, and they constantly used beatings, arson, threats, and outright murder to disrupt opposing political movements, particularly around election times. The Communists were not averse to dirtying their hands with slaughter in the name of international revolution either, but they were much weaker than the Nazis. They had played their hand early in attempting a coup in 1919, seeking to prompt an armed worker's revolution that would create a Soviet-style tyranny in Germany, but they were quickly crushed by the brutal Freikorps, a right-wing paramilitary organization comprised of many World War I veterans. As such, the Freikorps possessed formidable combat skills the Communists could not match.

The Freikorps continued to seek out and kill Communists or suspected Communists during the following decade, greatly reducing the power of the party in Germany. Though still something of a force to be reckoned with, by 1933, the KDP (German Communist Party) simply did not have the manpower to go toe-to-toe with the Nazis and hope to survive, either in the German Parliament or the rough and tumble of the streets. The Freikorps would eventually be purged by Hitler, with most of its leaders executed and its rank and file absorbed first into the SA and then into the SS, but in the meantime, it rendered a considerable service to the future Fuhrer.

Elections held in November 1932 reduced the Nazis' seats in the parliament to around a third, with the deficit being claimed by the Communists, and the next elections were slated for March 6, 1933, exactly one week after the burning of the Reichstag occurred. Hitler and Goering were in need of a crisis both to generate a reason for passing dictatorial emergency powers, and to prevent the Nazis from losing further ground to the hated communists in the Reichstag.

Meanwhile, in late 1932 and early 1933, the German government "was preparing a massive job-creation programme to relieve unemployment through the state provision of public works (Evans, 2005, 308)." The Nazis had a firm grasp of the fact that it was economic disaster that made their extreme agenda seem appealing to the people at large. Their window of opportunity was shrinking, and they had only a few months left before their power would likely begin to wane. The Nazi Party and Hitler understood this instinctively.

At this moment, President Hindenburg made an utterly fatal error for the future of Germany, Europe, and the world. To the half-senile Field Marshal, "it seemed more urgent than ever at this point to tame the Nazis by bringing them into government (Evans, 2005, 310)," and this in turn "led to a plan to put Hitler in as Chancellor, with a majority of conservative cabinet colleagues to keep him in check." (ibid). In brief, the scheme concocted by the President and his ministers was to keep the Nazis from achieving power by giving them some power, buttressed by a naïve faith that the tut-tutting of a handful of aged politicians would suffice to rein in a man with approximately 400,000 SA brownshirts and 100,000 SS men at his disposal. Thus, with a surreal misjudgment, Hindenburg placed the few Nazis admitted into the highest ranks of government in precisely those positions best suited to the establishment of a dictatorship and police state: "Only two major offices of state went to the Nazis, but both of them were key positions on which Hitler had insisted as a condition of the deal: the Ministry of the Interior, occupied by Wilhelm Frick, and the Reich Chancellery itself, occupied by Hitler. Hermann Goring was appointed Reich Minister Without Portfolio and Acting Prussian Minister of the Interior, which gave him direct control over the police in the greater part of Germany. The Nazis could thus manipulate the whole domestic law-and-order situation to their advantage." (Evans, 2005, 312).

Hitler had played his hand brilliantly, exploiting circumstances, popular conspiracy theories, desperation, and the doddering incapacity of Germany's highest civilian leader to position himself in an extremely advantageous situation. The Nazis sensed that victory was within their grasp. For a few weeks, the real possibility existed that their power would melt away as economic programs finally helped Germany out of its long depression and into a newer, more democratic future, but Hitler managed to maneuver himself into the Chancellorship at essentially the last moment. Had Hindenburg chosen a different man as Chancellor and the job-creation program gained some breathing room to pick up momentum, there exists a very real possibility that there never would have been a Third Reich, a Final Solution, or World War II.

The Nazis had every reason to celebrate their stroke of good fortune at the 11th hour, and the victorious National Socialists marked the occasion in a fashion which expressed their own fierce satisfaction with the outcome and also served as a propaganda demonstration to showcase their strength, energy, and high degree of organization. "That Hitler's appointment as Reich Chancellor was no ordinary change of government became immediately clear, as Goebbels organized a torchlit parade of brownshirts, Steel Helmets and SS men through Berlin, beginning at seven in the evening on 30 January 1933 and going on well past midnight." (Evans, 2005, 315).

Still, at this point, Hitler still remained a functionary in the democratically elected government of the Weimar Republic, so a final touch was needed to grant him the powers which would transform a powerful but constitutionally limited Chancellor into the Fuhrer who would seek to establish a "Thousand Year Reich" on the ashes of the old European system. A high-profile incident was needed to give the pretext for Hitler to grant himself emergency powers and complete the metamorphosis from rabble-rousing former corporal to dictator.

Whether it occurred by accident or design, the burning of the Reichstag building on the night of February 27, 1933 provided Hitler with the necessary excuse.

The Reichstag in August 1932

Chapter 3: February 27, 1933

The night of February 27 was an ideal one from the standpoint of an arsonist preparing to set fire to one of Germany's most important government buildings. The air temperature hovered around 20 degrees Fahrenheit, several degrees below the average February low for the region, ensuring that less people than usual were out and about. The presence of snow on the ground was also somewhat unusual, since snow often melts rather quickly in the mild climates of central Europe.

Other factors also favored the incendiary or incendiaries, regardless of whether the attack was carried out by a lone wolf, Nazi agents, or Communist revolutionaries. The late hour and the upcoming elections ensured that the structure was uncharacteristically abandoned, reducing the number of potential witnesses, meddlers, and casualties. "There was an election on and the Reichstag was not in session; many deputies were away campaigning, and the work of the building's staff slowed down after 9:00. Between the rounds of the lighting man at 8:45 and the Reichstag mailman at 8:50 or 8:55, and the first inspection of the night watchman at 10:00, no one would be moving about inside the building. For this hour or so the Reichstag would be quiet, and, presumably—apart from the porter at the north entrance—empty." (Hett, 2014, 10).

Of course, the absence of other persons ensured that once spotted, any activity in and around the building would be immediately deemed suspicious, especially by policemen. In fact, just such an individual was present at the time the fire was lit: Karl Buwert, who had been assigned to keep a lonely vigil over much of the Reichstag's perimeter. Though he likely expected a quiet, tedious period of sentinel duty, a very different situation ultimately emerged.

The darkness of that bitterly cold late winter night obscured both the policeman's view and that of later historians seeking to determine exactly who was seen on the premises of the Reichstag when it burned. Chief Constable Buwert's eventful evening began at approximately 9:10 p.m. when Hans Floter, a theology student, approached him in a state of great excitement and announced that he had heard a window breaking and had seen a man with a torch on a second story balcony preparing to enter the building. Floter then left for home while the Chief Constable investigated, and almost immediately, a second figure hurried towards him through the gloom. This proved to be a young newspaper typesetter named Werner Thaler, who reported a broken window on another area of the facade and the sighting of two men with torches entering through this opening.

Buwert and Thaler investigated together, plainly seeing the broken window the young man had mentioned. There was already a glow of light inside, and the typesetter later claimed to have seen two torches inside, likely indicating a pair of arsonists at a minimum. Buwert fired his pistol in the general direction of the torches, prompting their carrier or carriers to move deeper into the building to avoid his bullets.

Picture of the window through which the alleged arsonist broke in

Fire engines began arriving on the scene, and at this point, Thaler felt his presence was superfluous and left. However, "as he crossed the Platz der Republik he 'turned around one more time and noticed that the cupola of the Reichstag was brightly lit.' That could only mean a much larger fire in the plenary chamber at the center of the building. 'I ran back to the firemen and told them that the interior of the building was also burning.'" (Hett, 2014, 15 – 16).

Thaler was not the only individual to note the ominous glare of rising light emerging from the iron and glass cupola that capped the Plenary Chamber. The Reichstag was one of the city's larger buildings, and many lines of sight to it existed thanks to its isolated placement on the Platz der Republik. This was no minor fire but an all-out blaze that threatened to gut the Reichstag's whole interior. Though the stone shell would remain largely intact save where intense heat might crack a few stone blocks, the curtains, chairs, paneling, and carpets inside were all highly inflammable, as were the large numbers of documents stored on the site.

Two of the main actors in the whole political tragedy, Paul von Hindenburg and Franz von Papen, were very close by, sharing a leisurely meal at the "Herrenklub" ("Gentlemen's' Club"), which commanded a view of the Reichstag. Von Papen reported, "Suddenly we noticed a red glow through the windows and heard sounds of shouting in the street. One of the servants came hurrying up to me and whispered: 'The Reichstag is on fire!' which I repeated to the President. He got up and from the window we could see the dome of the Reichstag looking as though it were illuminated by searchlights. Every now and again a burst of flame and a swirl of smoke blurred the outline." (Shirer, 2011, 196).

The brilliant illumination of the fire in the Plenary Chamber shining through the glass windows of the cupola was visible even further away. Hermann Goering's valet, Robert Kropp, was sipping mint tea in his employer's apartment while Goering was absent, working late on Unter dem Linden at the police offices (a fact that might have had an ominous significance). The valet's relaxing evening alone was not destined to last, however, for "the telephone rang, and when he answered it Adermann, the night porter at the presidential palace, was on the other end. He was excited and shouted: 'You must tell the minister at once! The Reichstag is on fire!'" (Mosley, 195).

After telephoning Goering (who had already received a report from the police), Kropp "slipped on his coat and went out and across to the Reichstag, from the dome of which he could now see, as he approached, flames licking." (Mosley, 195). Therefore, three separate accounts from widely separated individuals show that fire and smoke were already visible in the Plenary Chamber's cupola within a few minutes of the initial alarm being raised. This is an important question when trying to determine whether chemical accelerants such as gasoline were used to hasten the spread of the fire.

The Plenary Chamber clearly blazed up rapidly, almost suddenly, at about the same time the windows were broken and Buwert fired his pistol at an unknown prowler or prowlers inside the Reichstag. Though accelerants seem the most likely cause, a similar effect of a sudden, large fire in an enclosed space could theoretically result from flashover. Flashover occurs when the substances in a closed room reach their ignition temperature at the same time that the air is filled thickly with flammable gasses emitted from heated objects. When this threshold is reached, the entire room ignites suddenly, vastly increasing the size of the fire in an instant. Sometimes, the effect is even explosive, in which case the phenomenon is known as a "smoke explosion." Such an event can be lethal to anyone in the room, and it could potentially explain how the Plenary Chamber fire metamorphosed from a dim glow into a bright inferno that resembled "searchlights" shining out of the dome, with flames massive enough to lick out of the windows

246 feet above the chamber floor in a matter of a few minutes.

That said, one salient fact renders a flashover implausible. Without large quantities of accelerants to hasten the process, a long burn would be needed to set up the proper conditions for such an event to occur. The Plenary Chamber was a large space, and considerable time would be needed for the surfaces to heat to the point of combustion and the huge gulf of air it contained to acquire a thick enough burden of flammable gasses to catch fire. There was insufficient time for a modest fire to expand to the point of flashover between 8:45 p.m. (when the lighting man came through the building) or the mail deliveries by the parliamentary building's mailman at 8:55 and the observed blaze at 9:15-9:20 p.m. Given that the use of accelerants was almost certainly needed to create such a daunting fire so quickly, and the conditions of the alleged lone arsonist's capture, it seems quite likely that several men were involved in the arson that night.

Police, firemen, and officials all quickly converged on the ominously burning Reichstag, where a desperate battle was soon underway to extinguish the colossal fire. Among the people who put in an appearance were Goering and Hitler himself. According to later accounts by Goering's valet Robert Kropp, Goering made an effort to reach his office in order to rescue his Gobelin tapestries, but he was driven back by fierce flames, his face blackened by soot and streaked with tears, the latter caused either by smoke irritation or sorrow at the destruction of the former air ace's favorite textile art.

Conversely, Hitler was in an exultant mood. As Goering emerged from the building and went to meet the Chancellor, "his faithful valet [...] was astonished to see the look of triumph, almost of pleasure, on Hitler's face. 'This is a beacon from heaven!' Hitler shouted, above the crackle of the flames." (Mosley, 196). Whether the fire was a serendipitous accident of timing or a deliberate act arranged at his instigation, Hitler clearly grasped what an opportunity the conflagration presented in the political arena. In the course of putting out the fire, a convenient culprit was also discovered wandering through the Reichstag's labyrinthine interior, and he promptly arrested by the swarms of police who had converged on the scene. This individual was Marinus van der Lubbe, a young man with Communist affiliations and Dutch origins who spoke very bad German. The arsonist was found shirtless, having used his upper garments as kindling for the fire he had no hesitation in admitting he had set, and he was carrying a box of matches. The police photographed him later holding this box, though by this time they had supplied him with a shirt and jacket to replace those he had incinerated in the depths of the Reichstag.

Van der Lubbe

No deaths or injuries resulted from the Reichstag fire, which occurred at a time when the building was empty save for the arsonist or arsonists. The solid stone construction eliminated the risk of collapse on the firemen and policemen who came to the scene, and they were careful enough to avoid any fatalities from direct fire exposure or smoke inhalation.

Slightly more than two hours after it began, the Reichstag fire was extinguished around 11:30 p.m., but by then, it had reduced practically the whole interior of the building to a charred shambles, destroying wood paneling, curtains, seats, lecterns, all manner of furniture, artworks, carpets, and reams of irreplaceable government documents and records. The fire went out due to a mix of intense efforts on the part of Berlin's firefighters and the fact that it had exhausted most of its potential fuel sources. The huge government building had been gutted, and it continued to send wisps of smoke upward into the icy air for days afterward.

A picture of ruins within the Reichstag

As the last smoldering ashes of the heaped wood and cloth inside cooled, however, a fire of a different kind had been lit in the hearts of the Nazi leadership. Feigning outrage against a Communist takeover plot of which there is scant to no evidence, the Nazis immediately began to exploit the Reichstag fire as a pretext for granting Hitler sweeping, unconstitutional powers, and for removing the Communists from the political scene as much as possible.

Chapter 4: The Nazi Response to the Reichstag Fire

"I'm convinced he was responsible for the burning of the Reichstag, but I can't prove it." – Adolf Hitler in reference to Communist Party chairman Ernst Togler

The National Socialist party's response to the Reichstag fire was quick and forceful, in part because the Nazis and the police (who were now under the supervision of Goering) appeared to be readying their organizations for some kind of trouble. Goering was out of his home working with police officials when the Reichstag fire occurred, even though it was relatively late in the evening, but this was not the only indication that the Nazis were prepared for some sort of triggering event to offer them a pretext for arresting large numbers of their political rivals. The Gestapo was a newly formed organization in 1933, created as a secret police at the same time

Hitler ascended to the Chancellorship on January 30, and the commander of this sinister new enforcement group was Rudolf Diels, a slippery figure who managed to avoid prosecution after World War II despite being neck deep in Nazi police state activities. In fact, the resourceful Diels, whose facial scars and icy, cynical gaze gave him the appearance of a villain from a Cold War spy thriller, actually wormed his way successfully into the postwar government of Lower Saxony.

Diels

Those days were remote in 1933, however. At that time, Diels made remarkable (and incriminating) preparations on the afternoon of January 27th, 1933, just a few hours before the fire at the Reichstag broke out. Making good use of early technology for coordinating his plan, the Gestapo leader "sent out an order by radio to all police stations in Prussia. 'Communists,' said Diels, were 'said to be planning attacks on police patrols and the members of national organizations' […] [and] 'suitable countermeasures' against the Communist threat were to be taken 'immediately.' Above all, 'in necessary cases' Communist functionaries were to be taken into 'protective custody.' By shortly after six that evening, all Prussian police stations had received Diels's order. Hours before fire consumed the Reichstag, the police were ready." (Hett, 2014, 39).

   Both Diels and Goering had drawn up extensive arrest lists of influential Communists and others who were vocally opposed to the Nazis' rising fortunes, and these lists were up to date and ready for action when the flames shone through the darkness from the Reichstag's glass-paneled cupola. It is even possible that Goering was out of his house that fateful evening putting the finishing touches to them and making certain that no crucial names had been omitted among those who were destined to experience the horrors of Nazi "protective custody."

   After his abortive attempt to rescue his Gobelin tapestries from the fire, Goering soon accosted Diels, who had also put in an appearance on the scene of the conflagration in record time. Most of the chief Nazi leaders of the day were at the Reichstag within minutes of the alarm being sounded, which made coordination of their ensuing actions remarkably quick and easy. Franz von Papen later provided a vivid account of the words Goering shouted at the Gestapo leader, for he had worked himself into a lather of rage and indignation by this time: "This is the beginning of the Communist revolution! We must not wait a minute. We will show no mercy. Every Communist official must be shot, where he is found. Every Communist deputy must this very night be strung up." (Shirer, 2011, 196).

   A quick death from a bullet or noose would likely have been a kindness compared to the actual fate of many of those on Diels' lists. The first arrests began almost immediately, though they were not to achieve their full momentum until early the next afternoon, when Hitler's position as dictator was firmly established by legal decree of the President and Reichstag of the Weimar Republic. Hitler seized the opportunity presented to him with both hands. Loudly and forcefully trumpeting his version of events – that the Reichstag fire was a signal for a Communist revolution which, curiously, showed no signs whatsoever of developing in reality – the Chancellor appeared before the gathered officials of the Weimar Republic at 11 a.m. on the morning of February 28 while the ashes of the Reichstag interior were still hot. Hitler was bearing a decree from the 1920s, originally drafted during an anti-communist panic, and an authoritarian fanatic, Ludwig Grauert (a man in the employ of Hermann Goering), had added extra material to it in the form of a second clause which made the powers it granted to the Chancellor even more sweeping and arbitrary. If it was approved and signed by President Hindenburg, it would more or less give Hitler almost unlimited power. Incredibly, Hindenburg's cabinet, frightened by the Reichstag fire and the bogeyman of Communist revolution, accepted the document and presented it to the President, though Franz von Papen expressed dismay at the idea and urged his colleagues to reject the proposal out of hand. Hindenburg showed remarkably little hesitation before signing the decree, propelling Hitler to the position of absolute dictatorship he was to occupy until he took poison along with Eva Braun in the fire-streaked darkness of Berlin a dozen years later in order to avoid capture and torture at the hands of the victorious Soviets.

The decree, which has gone down in history as the "Reichstag Fire Decree," suspended most of the democratic guarantees and rights in the Weimar Republic. "Thus restrictions on personal liberty, on the right of free expression of opinion, including freedom of the press, on the right of assembly and association, and violations of the privacy of postal, telegraphic and telephonic communications, and warrants for house-searches, orders for confiscations as well as restrictions on property rights are permissible beyond the legal limits otherwise prescribed." (Evans, 2005, 336).

This remarkable document went on to give Hitler the power to assume absolute power over any of Germany's states where such a measure was deemed "necessary," and it gave the Chancellor and those he delegated the power to inflict death penalties for the appallingly broad, vague crime of "disturbing the peace." This decree was to remain in effect "until further notice," which in practice meant forever, or at least until shells, bombs, and bullets broke the strength of the "Thousand-Year Reich." Hindenburg's signature was the suicide note of the Weimar Republic, and it marked the President's personal obeisance to the man he had very recently scorned as the "Bohemian corporal." A single signature put an end to the democratic experiment in Germany and ushered in 12 years of terror, murder, war, and one of the most brutal dictatorships in history.

Naturally, Hitler wasted no time in utilizing his freshly acquired totalitarian powers. The arrests that Diels and Goering had already begun now attained the color of authority and legality, and the SA joined with the police in a sweeping purge of the German population. The flails of legalized Nazi aggression winnowed the political field, removing the best candidates of opposing parties and leaving only the compliant Nazi party members in the legislature: "Some four thousand Communist officials and a great many Social Democrat and liberal leaders were arrested, including members of the Reichstag […] Truckloads of storm troopers roared through the streets all over Germany, breaking into homes, rounding up victims and carting them off to S.A. barracks, where they were tortured and beaten. [...] the Social Democrat newspapers and many liberal journals were suspended and the meetings of the democratic parties either banned or broken up." (Shirer, 2011, 198 -199).

Notably, although the official Nazi party line was the that Reichstag fire was caused by Communists as a signal for a Soviet-style revolution, the Social Democrats were arrested and tormented with equal zeal by the police and SA. The agenda of silencing all potential political opponents, including those who were in favor of democracy and did not even think of using extralegal force to attain their goals, became nakedly apparent less than 24 hours after Chief Constable Buwert fired his pistol at unknown prowlers in the Reichstag. The Nazis' preeminence in the elections of March 6th, 1933 had been assured in one bold, unscrupulous stroke.

Oppression of the Jews began almost immediately as well. The populace had been propagandized into blaming the Jews for Germany's defeat in World War I, shifting blame rather than accepting that Germans, like all other humans, had limitations despite their courage and intelligence and could be overwhelmed by a numerous, determined adversary. The Jews also made a convenient scapegoat for the subsequent financial miseries that racked Germany during the postwar years.

Ironically, it was the very helplessness of the Jews that made them a prime choice for targeting because of their "undue power" over the fate of Germany. Accused of being so powerful as to be able to bring down a formidable military power through practically invisible means, the Jews were somehow also so powerless that they could fall ready victims to the anger of the mob. The reality, of course, is that the Jews were a "safe" target for the people to take out their frustrations on. Representing less than 1% of the population, they did not have the numbers to resist hordes of Germans baying for their blood, and even before the rise of the Nazis, the government tacitly colluded with the anti-Semites by failing to properly protect its own Jewish citizens.

Hitler may indeed have convinced himself of the bizarre conspiracy theories about World War I, thus justifying denial of the unpalatable truth that the despised Allies had simply outfought the German army and defeated it. Whatever the case of his personal beliefs, the Jews made a convenient conduit for the fear and aggression of the German people, which might otherwise have been directed against the SA thugs running rampant over civil liberties. Regardless, beatings, rapes, and killings of Jews became norms that the authorities winked at, and on April 1, 1933, just a little over a month after the Reichstag fire, Hitler began a boycott of Jewish businesses intended to deprive his chosen victims of what little economic power they actually had. Jackbooted SA roughnecks posted signs in shop windows or loitered menacingly at the entrances to deter people from entering and buying from the proprietors. The measure was mostly a failure, but it served as an ominous warning of worse events to ensue.

One aspect of Hitler's rise to power which is frequently overlooked by modern historians was the massive program of disarmament and gun control which the Nazis instituted, confiscating private firearms in order to ensure their rule was undisputed. A far-flung campaign of search and seizure was started, with anyone found in possession of a gun classified as a "Communist" even though most of those afflicted in this manner were law-abiding Social Democrats. "The Nazis succeeded in creating a 'Communist gun owner' bogeyman to justify extensive searches and seizures conducted by the police to confiscate firearms and arrest their owners. To carry out these measures, some 5,000 auxiliary police composed of SA, SS, and Stahlhelm members were enrolled in Berlin alone." (Halbrook). Of course, the three Nazi organizations that backed Hitler – the SA, SS, and Steel Helmets – were not only permitted to keep their weapons but were armed with pistols and steel-shafted clubs by the government in cases where the men did not already possess such arms. Anyone who did not belong to these organizations, however, was apt to be arrested and placed in the concentration camps Hitler already found necessary to contain the hordes of undesirables he and his cronies alone seemed to be able to detect in the German population.

Given the robust tradition of shooting clubs in Germany, which stretched back as far as the "crossbow leagues" of the medieval era, the arrests that followed Hitler's strict gun control measures were extensive and occurred all across Germany. Though most of those arrested were later released, perhaps somewhat worse for wear, this measure did have the effect of removing armed male citizens not directly affiliated with the Nazi party from circulation at precisely the moment when popular resistance to the Fuhrer's takeover might have been effective. After all, these measures came before the Nazi state had truly consolidated its grip on Germany and acquired tanks and aircraft.

A second decree passed on March 24, 18 days after the Nazis won 44% of the seats in the Reichstag, completed the transition of Germany from the democratic experiment of the Weimar Republic to the personal fief of Adolf Hitler: "The Enabling Law – the popular name for the euphemistically-worded Law to Remove the Distress of the People and State – […] was the last nail in Weimar Republic's coffin […] Passed by the Reichstag, which then dissolved itself, the act provided that the cabinet could decree laws without consulting the Reichstag or the president. The chancellor – Hitler – was empowered to draft the laws, which could deviate from the Constitution." (Holbrook, 2013).

The burning of the Reichstag, whether it was a deliberate "false flag" operation or a random act of individual arson, was adroitly used as a springboard to absolute power by Hitler and his close clique of followers. The wily Fuhrer might have achieved supreme command over Germany by other means, but this is by no means certain. By having arrest lists prepared and the police, SA, and SS standing by even prior to the actual arson, the Nazis were positioned to severely disrupt the other major political parties on the eve of a crucial election.

Furthermore, the Reichstag fire created an atmosphere of paranoia and panic in which Hitler found it possible to force the passage of two decrees which gave him absolute authority over every level of German government and the life and death of every German citizen. The "Reichstag Fire Decree" of February 28 and the Law to Remove the Distress of the People and State of March 24 effectively abolished the law except as a manifestation of Hitler's will. Under the deeply flawed Weimar Republic constitution, this abolition was actually legal, which, along with the massive arrest program directed at non-Nazi gun owners during March 1933, served to utterly deflate any organized resistance to the Nazis' smooth and successful coup d'etat.

Chapter 5: The Trial of Marinus van der Lubbe and the Other Conspirators

Ironically, the trial held for the arsonist Marinus van der Lubbe and the other alleged conspirators were somewhat superfluous. Though the Nazis tried to use the trial to incriminate the Communists, the gesture was hollow by that point in time because the accused men did not come to trial until September 1933. By then, Hitler had already used the notion of a Communist takeover to stage his own dictatorial coup many months before, so the Fuhrer was monarch of Germany in all but name, and the Third Reich was well and truly launched. The prolonged and farcical trial in the autumn was clearly intended as a propaganda piece, but by then, it was no more than gilding on the lily. Hitler's political opponents had long since been shot, mauled physically by the SA, flung into early concentration camps, or otherwise silenced.

Five men in all were indicted for the Reichstag fire, even though the Nazis had portrayed them as the shock troops of a plot involving thousands of rabid Communist revolutionaries. The main suspect, of course, was Marinus van der Lubbe, the Dutch mason, Communist, and poser who had actually been found wandering about in the burning Reichstag with a box of matches obligingly in his hands. The 24 year old made no secret of his attempt to burn down the parliamentary building, and his existence must have delighted the Nazi authorities with its convenient serendipity.

The second defendant was Ernst Torgler, the head of the Communist caucus in the Reichstag who was arrested on the basis of this tenuous connection. The other three men were Bulgarian Communists, including Georgi Dimitrov, who proved himself intelligent, resourceful, and highly aggressive in turning the tables on his Nazi accusers. Dimitrov not only won his acquittal but fashioned a circumstantial case with his penetrating observations and questions for the Nazis that seemed to suggest the Nazis themselves were responsible for the burning of the Reichstag. Blagoi Popov and Vasil Tenev were also among the accused, but they played little role in the trial and depended on Dimitrov for their salvation.

Torgler

Dimitrov

The trial proceeded in normal German fashion, with a group of five judges who cross-examined witnesses themselves. The accused also spoke as their own advocates and called witnesses to support or refute various points. Though lawyers were present, they served mainly as advisers and legal references for their clients, but they did keep a sharp eye out for incorrect procedures which their clients would likely be ignorant of themselves.

The trial quickly developed into two parallel proceedings consisting of the spirited and incisive defense Georgi Dimitrov presented for himself and the three Communists accused alongside him, and the long, wretched cross-examination of Marinus van der Lubbe, who freely admitted his guilt from the start. The Nazis were eager to link all the men together and force them to admit to a huge Communist plot involving the whole German KDP. From first to last, they refused to countenance the idea that van der Lubbe set the fire alone, though this was the conclusion the court eventually reached.

Dimitrov handled his defense case with such vigor that he easily tore apart all of the charges brought against himself, Torgler, Popov, and Tenev. In the process, he managed to build a convincing though circumstantial case against the Nazis themselves as the incendiaries who had burned the Reichstag. For example, Dimitrov questioned why, if a Communist uprising was actually feared by the Nazis, they made no effort to mobilize soldiers or police forces on the night of February 27th to meet the supposed revolutionaries halfway. He pointed out, quite correctly, that far from making ready for battle, the Nazi leadership was relaxed and in control on the night of the Reichstag's burning.

Point after point was demolished by Dimitrov, and the Nazis interfered in the trial by removing Dimitrov from the courtroom several times to silence him. At times, they sent in both Goering and the notorious Nazi propaganda minister Joseph Goebbels to harangue the prisoner and intimidate him into making an error, but nothing could halt the Bulgarian Communist's defense. In fact, Dimitrov cross-examined Goering to such effect that he laid bare the former pilot's total ignorance of police procedure and uselessness as a police official.

Goebbels

A picture taken during the trial that includes Goering (standing)

Four of the men were ultimately acquitted of the accusations, a sign that the judges were attempting to be fair even while operating a court in Hitler's Germany and under extreme pressure to secure a guilty verdict that would implicate the whole Communist party in a plot centered on arson and uprising. Ernst Torgler was released but then arrested again immediately and placed into "protective custody." After a year and a half experiencing the truncheons of the brownshirts, Torgler became cooperative and began to work for the Gestapo in various roles. He was a Nazi official until the end of the war and later found work in the postwar government.

Georgi Dimitrov had made a name for himself, particularly in Communist circles, and he was named as the Premier of Bulgaria following the end of World War II. He was only in office for a few years, but during that time he demonstrated he possessed a level of brutality matching the Nazis'. He enforced the new Communist government with arbitrary arrests, torture, and executions, precisely the methods used by his former adversaries in Nazi Germany.

Van der Lubbe was left to face the brunt of the law's condemnation alone. Though his testimony hinted strongly that the Reichstag was already burning when he entered it, and that the fires he had not lit were already blazing around him when he set fire to his shirt, it is quite possible that the pyromaniac mason thought himself the sole author of the Reichstag fire, since publicity seeking and delusions of grandeur seemed to be goal. He had a long history of outlandish behavior and extraordinary, usually utterly false claims which, if true, would have made him one of the 20th century's most prolific arsonists and saboteurs. As one historian noted, van der Lubbe "was an avid publicity hound and had once tried to swim the English Channel without any preliminary training; […] he had a psychiatric record and pyromaniac tendencies; and […] he was inclined to claim credit for crimes, strikes, and sabotage, even when he was innocent." (Mosley, 196 – 197). In the aftermath of the Reichstag fire, the Communists themselves would try to portray van der Lubbe as unhinged.

Van der Lubbe was clearly guilty of at least some minor acts of arson in the Reichstag, but it remains difficult to imagine that he could have created such an unstoppable whirlwind of fire without any chemical accelerants whatsoever and no tools beyond a box of large matches and his own shirt as kindling, all within the space of perhaps 10-15 minutes. The volatility of an ordinary shirt is not high, and it is certainly insufficient to trigger a flashover in a huge wood-paneled council chamber in just a matter of a few minutes. Furthermore, the Dutch arsonist clearly relied more on enthusiasm and chance than a careful methodology or knowledge of fires, which makes his chances of such a massive success that much smaller.

Still, van der Lubbe was a Communist of sorts, and therefore he was potentially useful to the Nazi hierarchy as a propaganda weapon. Considering that van der Lubbe's personality, insofar as it has come down to the present day in records, bears every stamp of an irrational, drama-seeking crank, one might perhaps suppose that he chose to be a Communist more because it was "shocking" and dramatic than through any conviction or true understanding of Communist principles.

Despite the fact that the Dutchman was an ideal "patsy" for the Nazis' power grab, it is possible that he was drugged during his trial to eliminate any chance that he would say anything that would disturb the Nazis' theory of a far-flung Communist plot. Surviving photos of van der Lubbe from his trial show him standing with his head slumped forward on his chest, eyes closed, and mouth hanging. Written accounts confirm that this was his demeanor throughout the trial except on two occasions when he appeared slightly more alert and managed to provide semi-coherent statements in contrast to his typical vague rambling: "On all but two of the trial's fifty-seven days van der Lubbe appeared with his head bent down over his chest, often drooling or with his nose running so that his police attendants had continually to wipe his face. He spoke in monosyllables or not at all […] He repeatedly answered 'yes' and then 'no' to the same question. At best he answered questions only after a long pause. Sometimes he did not answer at all. Sometimes he giggled." (Hett, 2014, 127).

There is additional reason to believe that this grotesque farce involved use of drugs because of the precise correspondence of the Dutch mason's behavior to a person heavily dosed with the most frequently utilized sedative in Germany at the time. As one historian explained, "van der Lubbe's appearance and behavior during the trial were consistent with the symptoms of excessive ingestion of potassium bromide, which, in its trade application Cabromal, was one of the most common sedatives at the time. Potassium bromide, which tastes like salt, can easily be slipped into food; symptoms of its abuse include mental slowness, loss of memory, apathy, a constantly running nose, and a slumped body posture." (Hett, 2014, 150).

Since van der Lubbe, unlike the other prisoners, admitted to setting a fire in the Reichstag, his guilt was never really in question. However, despite his evident sedation, he always refused to implicate anyone else in his arson plot and insisted that he alone had been the author of it. This insistence probably stemmed not only from a powerful desire to lay claim to the distinction of being the lone wolf who had gutted the mighty Reichstag, but also to the fact that van der Lubbe probably did not know anyone else to blame. He could not supply the names of Communist supporters of his actions because he simply did not know them. This refusal to blame a wider Communist plot drove the Nazis wild and caused the trial to drag on endlessly as they hoped for a breakthrough confession that would support their version of events. Finally, even van der Lubbe said that being executed would be preferable to continuing the endless, pointless trial, and the judges obliged him by sentencing him to death by the guillotine. Several of the judges experienced poor health as a result of the trial's stresses, and one of them died shortly after the trial concluded.

Meticulously kept prison records show that although van der Lubbe was killed in a relatively merciful fashion, his life was dispensed with in a highly perfunctory manner, almost as though he were a useless piece of inanimate garbage being discarded. After van der Lubbe was brought into the execution courtyard, his crime and sentence were read, and he was then tied onto the board, positioned, and beheaded in less than 55 seconds. It is worth recalling that the crime he was executed for had caused no deaths or injuries and was, even if the highly improbable notion of his sole guilt was accepted, purely a crime against property. Eventually, van der Lubbe received a posthumous pardon from the German government in 2008. By its terms, van der Lubbe was not found innocent of the charge of arson levied against him, but his conviction and sentence were vacated because they were handed down by a totalitarian state, and their excessive nature marked them as an unjust oppression inflicted on the Dutchman in violation of his human rights.

Chapter 6: The Lingering Debate Over the Reichstag Fire

There is no doubt that the burning of the Reichstag was exceedingly convenient for the Nazi party and Hitler. The police and SA were mobilized earlier the same day in preparation for a sweeping series of arrests both of Communists and Social Democrat leaders, which is a highly incriminating circumstance. After all, if Marinus van der Lubbe was the only arsonist involved, Diels and Goering could not have known he was about to strike.

Furthermore, the burning occurred immediately before an election, with just enough time left to give the Nazis the necessary interval to capture most of their main adversaries. Hitler then adroitly transferred all power to himself and made his will superior to the Weimar Republic constitution, even while technically leaving it in place to give his reign the color of legal legitimacy, with the Reichstag Fire Decree and the Enabling Law. The SA sprang into action, imprisoning Communists, Social Democrats, and non-Nazi firearms owners in droves with fierce energy and a high degree of coordination.

Given the preparations and the aftermath, there is plenty to suggest that the arson at the Reichstag did not take the Nazis by surprise. Instead, they seemed fully prepared to exploit every opportunity it offered them in great detail. While this evidence is purely circumstantial, some physical evidence is also compelling in establishing a group of SA saboteurs as the chief arsonists in the Reichstag, including the short length of time available for van der Lubbe's burning shirt to start a massive fire. According to some estimates, the amount of time required for van der Lubbe to reach the Plenary Chamber after breaking in would have left a mere 150 seconds between the ignition of his shirt and the vast pyre that was sending tongues of flame out of the 246 foot high cupola. There is insufficient time for a flashover or smoke explosion to occur even with the most generous estimates of van der Lubbe's arson skills.

Furthermore, van der Lubbe did not bring accelerants with him and could not have carried them in sufficient amounts to produce the observed conflagration. He could have brought them in during multiple trips into the interior, but there was simply no time for this to happen. At the same time, several experienced firemen on the scene testified to seeing burn trails indicating that gasoline or another accelerant had been poured along the floor: "One of the supporting judges […] took up the matter of the gasoline on the carpet. The trail ran from one door to the other, said [the fireman named] Gempp; a few stretches of carpet along the trail were "completely burned out." Gempp had bent down to smell the carpet, and believed that it had been gasoline or benzene [Benzin oder Benzol], [...] Lateit also testified to seeing a fire on a runner that led from the lobby into the plenary chamber, and described another fire running in a line against the wall, which at first he took for floor lighting." (Hett, 2014, 135 to 136). Such claims are consistent with the size, power, and rapidity of the fire, and they also rule out van der Lubbe as the sole arsonist.

Ultimately, a Nazi-intimidated court failed to find the slightest evidence of a Communist plot to burn the Reichstag, and subsequent seizures of the Communist party papers by the SA was also unable to turn up any reference to an arson scheme. Conversely, verbal testimony exists to implicate the Nazis. During the weeks prior to the blaze, Karl Ernst, the leader of the Berlin SA at the time, was seen frequently in Goering's official residence, which was connected to the Reichstag by a tunnel that passed under the street. Ernst, later accused of being a rapist and pedophile, was personally hated by Goering, so his presence in Goering's home was unlikely to have been a social call. Ernst always appeared with a small group of SA enforcers on these occasions, and he would be murdered in the notorious Nazi purge known as the Night of the Long Knives in 1934.

Ernst

Other suspicious nocturnal activity in the tunnel itself was confirmed by the night porter at Goering's house, Paul Adermann. This is the same individual who, on the night of the burning of the Reichstag, placed a panicky call to Robert Kropp, Goering's valet, to announce that the parliamentary building was in flames. Adermann stated that he had heard footsteps indicating unauthorized access of the tunnel in the late evening or early morning for up to a month before the fire occurred.

Not content with simply listening, Adermann had experimented to obtain concrete proof of whether or not the tunnel was being accessed by parties unknown late at night. "Adermann put wood chips on the floor of the tunnel and thin strips of paper across the tunnel doors at night— red strips on the red door and black strips on the black door so that they were inconspicuous. If anyone passed through the tunnel, the wood chips would be disturbed or the paper strips torn. 'How often did you find them torn?' Torgler asked. 'About six times' was the answer." (Hett, 2014, 133). If Adermann was telling the truth (and he had no motivation to tell lies), the tunnel between Goering's official residence and the Reichstag had been accessed more than half a dozen times by unknown persons entering it for unspecified purposes at an hour when they were unlikely to encounter anyone. Adermann's failure to confront the intruders also hints that he may have known precisely who they were and feared that he would die if he sought to challenge them. Instead, he collected information indirectly and kept well clear of the tunnel after dark.

Taken together, there is much to suggest that the suspicions of the time may have been well-founded. In this scenario, Karl Ernst and several of the men he trusted spent weeks moving a large quantity of accelerants into the service tunnel, where the chance of discovery was minimal. On the chosen night, Karl Ernst and his sabotage squad could have quickly moved from the tunnel into the Reichstag, avoiding the mailman and other service personnel operating on a fixed schedule. Once inside, they drenched the carpets and desks, and possibly the walls, with gasoline, phosphorous, and whatever other incendiary materials they chose to use.

The men then moved quickly through the building, using torches to light the accelerants. In fact, a burning torch was found under a table in the Reichstag by the firemen, and it almost certainly could not have been left by van der Lubbe. It is possible that some of the windows were broken simply to let in more air in order to make the fire burn faster and hotter. Buwert may have seen some of these men, and after he fired his pistol ineffectually at them, they could have retreated back into the tunnel, leaving the fire to quickly blossom out of control.

Since Ernst was murdered in the wake of Hitler's quashing of the SA in 1934 during the Night of the Long Knives, he was also effectively silenced. Several other men rumored to have participated in the Reichstag fire also quickly turned up dead, which may have been the Nazis' way of tying up loose ends that might prove embarrassing down the road.

That said, those who believe the Reichstag fire was a Nazi false flag operation continue to struggle to explain van der Lubbe's appearance on the scene. According to them, the presence of another arsonist on the scene was not what the Nazis were expecting and has distorted the historical record ever since, but finding the shirtless Dutchman wandering through the corridors with matches in hand and a willing confession on his lips must have appeared to be a stroke of luck equal to winning a lottery. However, even in this case, the plans of the Nazis went awry when van der Lubbe refused to endorse their theory of a far-reaching Communist plot.

Many conspiracy theories regarding false flag attacks are ludicrous and illogical, but in the case of the burning of the Reichstag, however, witness testimony, science, and common sense all seem to indicate that van der Lubbe could not have been the main arsonist and was merely a dabbling amateur lighting a small fire while the professionals around him started the chief blaze.

In the end, regardless of whether it was van der Lubbe, Karl Ernst and his stormtroopers, or some other party who set the main fire in the Reichstag, there is a certain symbolic appropriateness that Hitler was almost literally anointed upon the ashes of democracy. The Reichstag was the heart of the Weimar Republic's attempt at representative government and bore the inscription "The German People" above its main entrance. Hitler's ascent to power came over the scorched wreck of the building representing political freedom and the people themselves.

Chapter 7: The Soviets and the Reichstag

Long left as an abandoned, echoing shell, the Reichstag building played one final role in the dark saga of Hitler and Nazi Germany. The Soviets were impressed by the iconic image of six U.S. Marines raising the American flag on Iwo Jima and wished to create their own version of the scene. As Berlin fell to the Soviet juggernaut, the photographer Yevgeny Khaldei set about making his own iconic image with the Reichstag as the setting. Khaldei could not find a flag of sufficient size and was forced to attach pieces of three tablecloths together to make a suitably impressive hammer and sickle banner. He then enlisted the first three soldiers he found to help him: a Ukrainian named Alexei Khovalyov, a Belorussian called Leonid Gorychev, and a Dagestani named Abdulkhakim Ismailov. One of the men was wearing a second wristwatch on his right arm, which compelled the Soviet censors to paint it out since it constituted evidence of looting.

From a symbolic viewpoint, the choice of venue was appropriate. The Nazis had left the Reichstag vacant, despising it as an emblem of liberal democracy, and Khaldei's photograph inadvertently but fittingly encapsulated the fact that rather than being liberated, the eastern portions of Germany and much of Berlin itself had just fallen within the sphere of influence of another brutal totalitarian power. Indeed, the suffering of Germany was far from over after Hitler's fall.

The Reichstag in June 1945

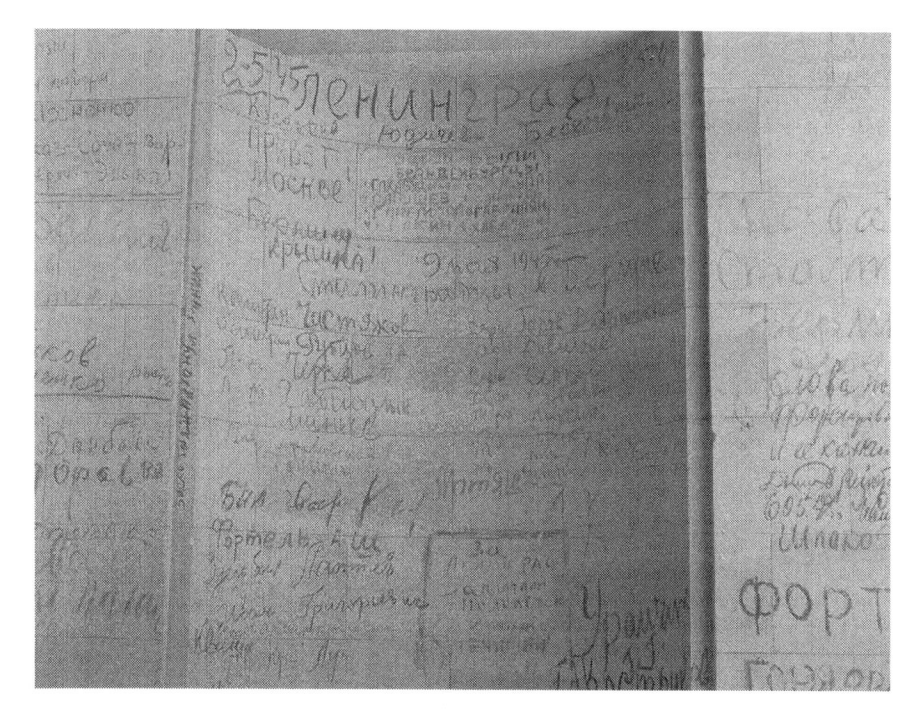

A picture of Soviet graffiti placed on the Reichstag building

Bibliography

Addington, Scott. *The Third Reich: A Layman's Guide.* Online/Amazon, 2014.

Berlin Online. *Reichstag.* Online, 2014.
  http://www.berlin.de/orte/sehenswuerdigkeiten/reichstag/index.en.php

Evans, Richard J. *The Coming of the Third Reich.* New York, 2005. (Reprint.)

Goldstein, Phyllis. *A Convenient Hatred: The History of Antisemitism.* Brookline, 2012.

Hett, Benjamin Carter. *Burning the Reichstag: An Investigation into the Third Reich's Enduring Mystery.* Oxford, 2014.

Holbrook, Stephen P. *Gun Control in the Third Reich: Disarming the Jews and "Enemies of the State."* Oakland, 2013.

James-Chakraborty, Kathleen. *German Architecture for a Mass Audience.* 2000.

Mosley, Leonard. *The Reich Marshal: A Biography of Hermann Goering.*

Shirer, William L., and Rosenbaum, Ron. *The Rise and Fall of the Third Reich: A History of Nazi Germany.* (Electronic edition.) New York, 2011.

Made in the USA
Columbia, SC
02 January 2025